C000258875

A BOOT UP

The Tamar Valley

Terry Faull

First published in Great Britain in 2010

British Library Cataloguing-in-Publication Data
A CIP record for this title is available from the British Library

ISBN 978 1 906887 64 3

PiXZ Books
Halsgrove House, Ryelands Industrial Estate,
Bagley Road, Wellington, Somerset TA21 9PZ
Tel: 01823 653777
Fax: 01823 216796
email: sales@halsgrove.com

An imprint of Halstar Ltd, part of the Halsgrove group of companies
Information on all Halsgrove titles is available at: www.halsgrove.com

Printed and bound by Toppan Leefung Printing Ltd, China

Contents

About this book

As rivers go the Tamar is rather a modest waterway. From its source on the moors close to the north Cornish coast, it runs less than 50 miles before emptying into the sea at Plymouth Sound. However, its lack of length is more than compensated by the scenery and the richness of the human and natural history to be found along its banks. The ten walks in this Book invite you to explore the Tamar Valley along the tidal reaches in the south and also excursions in the higher parts of the Valley to see ancient churches and farms and places rich in wildflowers and birdsong.

The Routes

Some of the walks are away from places promoted in popular tourist guides and your fellow walkers are likely to be local people who will be glad to share their favourite territory with you. Others follow more familiar pathways but the commentary will draw attention to features along the way which you may otherwise miss. Distances vary but none is more than five miles long and each walk is designed for those who enjoy a leisurely amble (and to stop to quietly enjoy the beauty and history of this special Valley) rather then someone who likes to set a pace to cover long distances.

The walks mostly follow public rights of way or land open for access. In a few cases, in order to complete a circular route, it has been necessary to include short stretches of roadway open to all traffic. These lanes are narrow and sometimes carry farm traffic or speeding motorists, so please take care.

There is a sketch map at the start of each walk and information about the terrain to be covered, parking and other facilities. Grid references are included to help you locate the start of the walk on an Ordnance Survey map — the Tamar Valley is covered by OS Explorer Maps 108,112 and 126 and readers are advised to use these maps in conjunction with this book.

The River Tamar

The river itself has its own myths and legends. One story tell of two giants who fought for the affections of a beautiful nymph called Tamara who lived in the waters close to its source; another tale confirms that the devil would never cross the Tamar into Cornwall in case he was caught and put in a pasty! The Romans knew the river as Tamaris and the Vikings sailed up on the tide to Calstock where they disembarked and made their way inland along Danescombe Valley to plunder the Saxon mint town of Lydford and then Tavistock Abbey. Later, the native Cornish allied themselves with yet more raiding Danes and in 838AD they combined to fight against the Saxons on Hingston Down overlooking the Tamar. The Saxons triumphed but there was an uneasy peace; in 927AD King Athelstan sought to ease hostilities by proclaiming the Tamar to be the boundary between his Anglo-Saxon Wessex and Celtic Cornwall.

Once a boundary between two countries, the Tamar still divides Devon from Cornwall. In this Book there are walks on both sides of the river so be sure to check which one you are on before debating with the locals!

Cargreen

Key to Symbols Used

Level of difficulty:

Easy

Moderate

More Challenging

Map symbols:

🚗	Park & start
——	Tarred Road
- - -	Footpath
– – –	Walk Footpath
■	Building
+	Church
▲	Triangulation pillar or other landmark
🚻	WC
🍴	Refreshments
🍺	Pub

Walk Locations

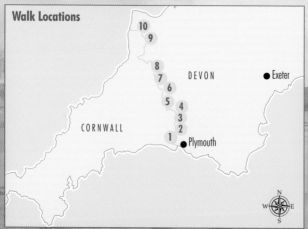

DEVON

CORNWALL

● Exeter

● Plymouth

N W E S

1 Landulph to Cargreen

The resting place of a Byzantine soldier of fortune, a pilgrim's port and a paradise for bird watchers.

Level:
Length: 2.5 miles
Terrain: Muddy foreshore and fields with one steep section
Parking: By Landulph church
Start Ref: Explorer Map 108 432615
Refreshments: Crooked Spaniard Inn. Cargreen.

Landulph means "sacred place of St Delch" (or "Deloc") one of the Celtic travellers who brought Christianity to this area in the 7th century. The Tamar is at its widest here and fully tidal so the state of the tide will determine whether it is possible to follow the path which runs along the foreshore or if it will be necessary to walk to Cargreen across the fields.

Cargreen riverside park

Landulph church

1. Park in the lay-by next to Landulph church and then take a little while to admire this ancient building which contains the remains of Theodore Palaeologus, the last descendent of the emperors of the Byzantine Empire. He came to this area after fighting on the side of the king during the English Civil War.

2. From the church gate walk along the drive to the left for about 300 metres to a stile on the right leading into a Cornwall Wildlife Trust Nature Reserve. Climb the stile and follow the pathway which skirts an area known as The Marsh. This was created when a Victorian rector built a wall to enclose an inlet of the estuary. The sea once came almost to the churchyard walls and in the Middle

Path beside the Marsh

Ages, pilgrims for the Holy Land embarked at Landulph for the perilous sea journey to the Mediterranean. The cleric's endeavours met with little success and plans to sell the water from the holy well and to develop a healing spa came to naught when sea water tainted the well. The land now lies mostly wet and boggy and is a haven for wildlife.

3. On reaching the sea wall the estuary is spread before you. In the distance you can see the suburbs of Plymouth and the road and railway bridges which span the Tamar. So close to the busy city yet here is a peaceful haunt of avocets, curlews and many wading birds who find rich feeding on the tidal mudflats.

Tamar bridges from Landulph

Foreshore path sign

(4) A sign points along the footpath which runs upstream and along the foreshore. This route can only be safely taken during the times of low spring tides (spring tides occur shortly after every Full and New Moon throughout the year and not just in the spring). There are two high and two low water periods every 24 hours, so if you have timed your visit at a low Spring tide, it may be possible to follow the muddy path close to the river bank.

(5) To avoid the muddy foreshore and if there are any doubts about the state of the tide, return to the church and walk up the road past

the car park. After a few hundred
yards and just as the hill gets steeper,
a footpath sign on the right directs
you along a narrow track which leads
to a stile into a field. After the stile,
follow the path alongside the left
hand hedge until you come to another
stile which you takes you down hill
across the middle of the field. From
here there are splendid views across
the river and down into the village of
Cargreen. A stile and gate takes you
into a lane leading down to a road
and a small park next to the river.

(6) The muddy walk along the
foreshore also brings you
here. The way into Cargreen is now
either along the river bank to a point
where an opening between the
gardens and houses leads up to the

Cargreen

street or, to avoid the mud and the tide, along the road and turn right down to the river's edge. Cargreen comes from the Cornish words meaning "seal rock" but you need to be very lucky to see such a creature this far up river.

(7) Cargreen was once connected to the opposite (Devon) side of the river by a ferry. This took baskets of local fruit and flowers across to the railway at Bere Ferrers Station and so on to London. To return to your car you have a choice of routes; the warnings about the foreshore path still apply and the alternatives are to follow the path back across the fields or to take the road up through the village, turn left into Church Lane and then left down to Landulph.

The Spaniards Inn and the river

2 Bere Ferrers and Weir Quay

Along an old school path, past an ancient landing place and beside remnants of an industrial past.

The parish of Bere Ferrers is sandwiched between the rivers Tamar and Tavy indeed the picturesque church is situated right on the water's edge. In earlier times there were a number of small working quays along both rivers but these have long been abandoned and today only pleasure boats and sailing craft ply the tidal waters.

Level: ♥♥
Length: 4.5 miles
Terrain: Fields and foreshore with a couple of steep hills
Parking: At Bere Ferrers station
Start Ref: Explorer Map 108 452635
Refreshments: The Olde Plough Inn, Bere Ferrers.

Tamar Valley Apple blossom

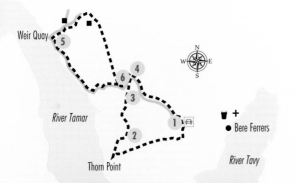

Weir Quay
5
4
6
3
River Tamar
1
● Bere Ferrers
2
Thorn Point
River Tavy

1 The start is at Bere Ferrers station which looks is if it has been taken out of *The Railway Children* and where Thomas the Tank engine can often be seen parked in a siding. Leave the station car park and turn right, after a short way turn right again and follow the road until you come to a railway bridge. Pass under the bridge and take the track ahead, continue over a stile and across the field to the far gate which takes you into a field with views of the river. Keep close to the wire fence on the left and walk down to a gate leading on to the riverbank. You are now close to Thorn Point, the landing place for the ferry across the Tamar from Cargreen and from where children would walk to the station to travel into schools in Plymouth.

2 At the gate leading to Thorn Point, turn right along the field bottom and close to the salt marshes of the river. On reaching a stile, climb over and make your way through a boggy area and across a timber walkway and bridge. The ruined buildings on the right of the path are the remains of a medieval settlement called Egypt and there are still old fruit trees left from that time. Continue through the field with the riverbank on your left until you reach a gate where signs explain the option of continuing along the footpath close to the water or, to avoid the mud, to follow a permissive path around the top of the cottages.

Bere Ferrers Station

The river

Footpath and stile at Liphill

3 The riverbank path takes you in front of Liphill cottages. This was once a tiny port and also where Tavistock Abbey had ponds which held water from high tide and used to extract salt. The lower path and the permissive route both lead on to the driveway where you should take the gate on the left. With Liphill Creek on the left, continue over three stiles.

4 Ahead you will reach a small stream which flows out of a stone bridge over a road which you reach up some convenient wooden steps. This is Tuckham, turn left here and follow the road up over the crest of the hill and then down to the river at Clamoak Quay.

5 Follow the road close to the water's edge to Weir Quay

slipway and the Yacht Club. Soon after passing Cleave Farm and a boat yard, turn right and continue uphill. On the left are buildings which were originally built as a smelting works for the ore from the Tamar Valley mines and a reminder of the industrial past of the valley. Past a red telephone box on the left and a Woodland Trust site on the right and continue up a rather steep

River at Clamoak

Weir Quay

hill until you see a signpost for Cotts pointing to the left with a farm lane to Lower Birch on the right. Take the farm lane and follow this all the way to where it joins a road where you turn downhill shortly to reach Tuckham bridge.

6 From here you can choose to retrace your steps across the fields, to continue along the road until you see a footpath sign down the drive to Liphill or to keep to the road which will lead back to Bere Ferrers station.

Distant Tamar bridges